CHRISTMAS TREES
and How They Grow

To a Christmas Tree

O balsam tree, that lately held
The stars like nesting birds among
Your emerald branches, listen now
To children's voices sweet with song!

You talker with the wind, and friend
Of fox and fawn and silver mouse,
Bearing your tinsel and your gifts,
Glow softly now within this house,

Bringing your fragrance to our hearts,
Assuring us that wars will cease.
For a Child's bright birthday shine with faith,
O tree of loveliness and peace!

From *The Little Whistler*, by Frances Frost

CHRISTMAS TREES

AND HOW THEY GROW

GLENN O. BLOUGH
PICTURES BY JEANNE BENDICK

3735

582
B

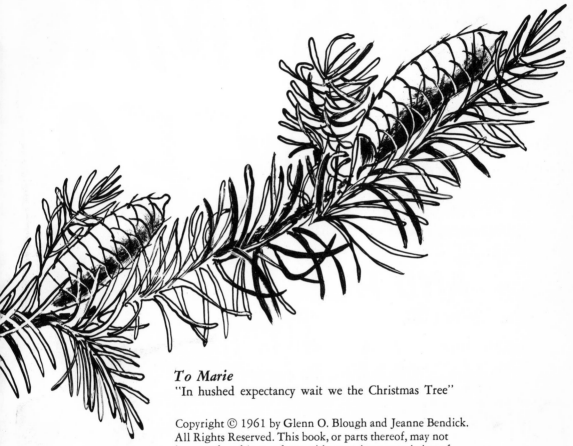

To Marie
"In hushed expectancy wait we the Christmas Tree"

Copyright © 1961 by Glenn O. Blough and Jeanne Bendick.
All Rights Reserved. This book, or parts thereof, may not
be reproduced in any form without written permission of
the publishers.

Library of Congress Catalog Card Number: 61: 15906

Printed in the United States of America

Third Printing

McGRAW-HILL BOOK COMPANY
New York   Toronto   London

T2-PL89-10

LIBRARY ST. ROSE OF LIMA SCHOOL
HOUSTON INDEPENDENT SCHOOL DISTRICT

FINDING
A CHRISTMAS TREE

Mr. Ball opened the gate for Billy and Barbara and they skipped through into the lane. They were on their way to the woods to find a Christmas tree.

"Dad, I wonder if we will see that fox squirrel again," said Billy.

"I doubt it," said his father. "It's too snowy and cold today. He's probably in his nest of leaves or in a hole in a tree."

"When will he find those cones we saw him hide last September?" asked Barbara. "They must be covered with snow now."

"Oh, probably on some warmer day when the snow melts. Or if he gets hungry enough he may even dig down under the snow," answered Mr. Ball. "What kind of a Christmas tree shall we get this year? I think you are big enough to help choose one."

4

"Let's get a straight, tall one," said Billy. "We don't want a lopsided one."

"This place looks like a picture on a Christmas card," said Mr. Ball when they reached the woods. "I like Christmas with snow."

Snow covered the ground and rested on the branches of the trees and bent them down a little. Everything was white and green and quiet.

White pines have long,
blue-green needles,
five in a cluster, with
long, narrow, thin-scaled
cones.

"Let's look for a tree with cones on it like the one we had last year," said Barbara. "Remember how nice the cones looked with the lights and balls and bells and things?"

"There are lots of trees to choose from," said Mr. Ball. "We can get a fir or a cedar or a spruce. They all grow in our woods. We might even get a white pine. There are a few white pines, I think."

"I don't know what firs and cedars look like," said Barbara. "We had a spruce last year, and I remember that its needles were sort of sharp and the cones were brown. It lasted a long time. I remember that."

"It was a white spruce," said Mr. Ball.

Black Spruce   White spruce

The cones of spruce trees
hang down. Their needles
are four-sided.

Balsam firs have flat, blunt needles, which stay on for a long time after the tree is cut. The cones are smooth and even and stand upright.

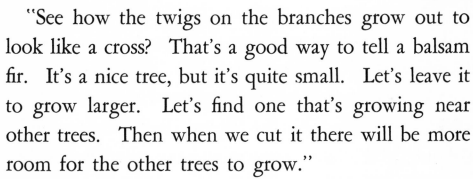

"I remember that it had a blue-green color," said Billy. "I liked it."

"There's a balsam fir," said Mr. Ball, pointing to a tall dark-green tree. "They make good Christmas trees." He showed Barbara and Billy the short flat needles.

"See how the twigs on the branches grow out to look like a cross? That's a good way to tell a balsam fir. It's a nice tree, but it's quite small. Let's leave it to grow larger. Let's find one that's growing near other trees. Then when we cut it there will be more room for the other trees to grow."

"Here's a nice tree," said Billy. "Wouldn't it be a good one?"

"That's a Douglas fir," said Mr. Ball. "See how the needles grow all the way around the twigs, instead of just on two sides as they do on some of the other fir trees?"

The needles of a Douglas fir grow in spirals around the twig. Each cone scale has a narrow, three-pointed bract growing from it.

7

Douglas firs that grow in thick forests are very tall, with long, bare trunks.
Douglas firs that grow in more open places have branches right to the ground.

"It's a beautiful tree," said Barbara. "Let's take it. It looks so pretty in the snow."

"Well, we can't take the snow with us," said Billy with a grin. "But I'll bet the tree is just tall enough to hold a star at the very top and not quite touch the ceiling in our living room."

"And look at those beautiful cones at the very top," said Barbara. "Please let's take this one."

"I think you have made a fine choice," said Mr. Ball, and he got the axe ready to cut the tree.

"It even smells like Christmas," said Barbara.

"My feet are cold," Barbara said as they started back down the lane.

"So are mine," said Billy. "But I'm glad we have such a nice tree."

"This is just like taking some of the woods right into our house," said Mr. Ball while he carried the tree down the lane to the gate.

"We didn't see the squirrel," said Barbara.

"We didn't even see any tracks," said Billy.

"Last night's snow covered them all up, I guess," said Mr. Ball. "I always think that Christmas begins when we find a Christmas tree," he said as he closed the gate to the lane.

While Barbara and Billy and Mr. Ball were busy finding a Christmas tree for their house, other people were busy getting another—much larger—tree ready. It was a tree for them and for everybody else in the United States. It was the National Community Christmas Tree in Washington, D.C. Barbara and Billy and their father and mother lived nearby, so they always went to see it. Mrs. Ball always said, "My Christmas begins when we go down and watch the President of the United States light the Christmas tree." Thousands of other people feel this way, too.

Maybe you, too, think that Christmas begins when you get your own Christmas tree. Many people do.

Did you ever wonder how a Christmas tree itself begins? If you had been with Billy and Barbara on the September day that they watched the fox squirrel in the woods, you might have discovered how Christmas trees sometimes start. What do you suppose happened?

GATHERING CONES

It was a fine September day in Mr. Ball's woods the day Barbara and Billy and their father watched the fox squirrel.

Fox Squirrel was busy. Down the pine tree he hurried with a pine cone in his mouth. He scurried over the ground, jumped over a log, and ran under a bush. Scratch. Scratch. Scratch. He covered the pine cone with brown needles and fallen leaves. Then back he went to the tree.

Up the tree, then down, hurry, scurry, jump, run, scratch, and he covered another cone with needles and leaves. He worked longer than a whole school day. He must have covered a half bushel of cones, or maybe even more. Autumn days are busy days for fox squirrels and many of the other animals that live in the woods.

When winter comes Fox Squirrel will look for his store of cones. Maybe he will find the cones. Maybe he won't. Maybe some other squirrel will find them. Maybe a chipmunk or even a small mouse will find them.

If Fox Squirrel finds the cones under the needles and leaves he will sit down and take one of the cones in his front paws and begin to take it apart.

Cones are made of scales that fold over each other. Under the scales there are tiny seeds. Fox Squirrel likes these seeds. He starts to work. Off come some

scales. Out come some seeds. And Fox Squirrel eats them. Off come more scales. Out come more seeds and Fox Squirrel eats them. For a hungry fox squirrel on a cold snowy winter day what could taste better than seeds from a pine cone? Hardly anything.

But if Fox Squirrel doesn't find the pine cones, or if a chipmunk doesn't find them, or if a small mouse doesn't find them, they may stay covered up. The cones with the seeds inside will get dry and brown. After a while the scales will open up and the pine seeds may slip out of the dry brown cone and slide down between the leaves and the needles to the ground. Then, if Fox Squirrel or a chipmunk or a small mouse does not find the seeds, something else may happen. They may start to grow.

Do you suppose that when Fox Squirrel covered the pine cones he might have planted a seed that will grow into a tree? Do you suppose he might even have planted a Christmas tree? Maybe a fox squirrel planted the seed that grew into the Christmas tree that Mr. Ball cut for Billy and Barbara. Maybe a fox squirrel planted your Christmas tree or the Christmas tree in your city, or maybe he planted the National Community Christmas Tree. He might have. Who knows?

On the same autumn day that Fox Squirrel was so
busy gathering pine cones, men were busy in a large
forest nearby. They were gathering cones and putting
them into big baskets. They gathered hundreds and
hundreds and hundreds of cones. They went to other
forests and gathered more cones there too. They gathered pine cones and cones from fir and spruce and
balsam trees too. But they didn't save them for winter as Fox Squirrel did. They took them to a Forest
Tree Nursery where small trees are grown to plant in
forests.

Hundreds and hundreds and hundreds of tiny seeds are planted in fields where the soil is just right for tree-growing. When the trees are big enough they are taken from the nursery and planted in a forest. Sometimes they are used to start new forests. Sometimes they are planted in forests where trees have been cut down or where a fire has burned them down. Sometimes they are planted in the same forest where the seeds came from.

Maybe your Christmas tree came from a seed that began to grow in a Forest Tree Nursery. It might have.

LIBRARY ST. ROSE OF LIMA SCHOOL

SPROUTING SEEDS

In the Forest Tree Nursery the cones are warmed to make them dry faster. The seeds won't come out of the cones until the cones are brown and dry. When they are dry enough, the scales begin to open. Then the cones are put into a machine that shakes them up and down and tumbles and tosses them around and around. Out come the seeds.

The seeds are very small. It takes a lot of them to make a hungry squirrel's dinner. It takes a lot of them to start a nursery to grow more trees to plant more forests to grow more cones to make more seeds too. If you looked at one of the tiny seeds you might say, "Can a big Christmas tree really grow from such a tiny seed?" Well, it can, and it takes only one tiny seed to grow up into a tall, beautiful tree. But it takes a long, long time.

 seed coat

If you look at the outside of the seed you will see the seed cover or seed coat. Some seeds have brown coats. Some have green coats. Some tree seeds have tiny wings fastened to them. When the seeds slip out of the cone on the trees they begin to fall to the

ground. If there is a small breeze it blows against the tiny wings and sends the seed drifting away. If there is a stiff wind it sends the seed sailing far away. The small breeze and a stiff wind both carry the seeds away from the tree to a new place. So if the lively squirrels don't carry the seeds to a new place, or if men from the nursery don't gather the seeds, the wind may carry the seeds to a place where they can grow. Maybe the seed that grew into your Christmas tree was carried by the wind to the place where it grew. Who can tell?

When you look at a seed it is hard to believe that it is alive. But if you put it in the ground the seed will begin to grow. When rain falls on the ground, it seeps down until it gets to the seed and then seeps in. The rain makes the seed coat soft. The sun shines on the ground and makes it warm. Now if you could see the seed you would know that it is alive. If you looked at the seed with a magnifying glass you would see the beginning of a tiny tree. It won't look like a Christmas tree with a trunk and leaves and branches. It's too small to look like anything you have ever seen, but just wait a month or so. Then it will look a little more like a tree.

The inside of the seed begins to get larger. It pushes on the seed coat. Slowly, slowly, it grows a little larger. Then the seed coat splits open. One part pushes down into the dark ground. This part is the root. One part pushes up into the sunlight. This part will be the trunk, with leaves and branches.

The tiny tree grows a little larger. The part in the sunlight grows green. It begins to grow taller. The part in the ground grows longer. It branches out and makes tiny roots that get water from the ground. This is the way your Christmas tree began. This is the way all Christmas trees begin.

If you can find some seeds from a dry cone you can sprout them and see for yourself how Christmas trees begin. Put the dry seeds on a piece of moist blotting paper so they will stay moist. After they sprout, plant them in dirt and you may start your own Christmas tree. But it will take a very long time to grow. Most kinds of Christmas trees are only a few inches high when they are a year old. It takes three or four years before some kinds are big enough to use for a table Christmas tree. It takes five or six years for trees to grow large enough to use for a Christmas tree in a schoolroom.

GROWING TREES

Trees have buds and flowers and leaves and branches and trunks and roots. These are the parts of a tree, and each part of a tree does something very important that makes the tree grow.

Let's suppose we could look down under the ground where the roots are. What's going on here? Down, down, way down in the ground are the tips of the roots. The tip of the root is the place where roots grow longer and push farther into the ground and spread out farther away from the tree.

The roots spread out and hold the tree. Strong winds blow against the branches and sometimes bend them low, but the roots keep the tree from tipping over. Roots are strong. They hold on to the ground where they are growing. If you try to pull up even a small tree you soon feel how well the roots hold the tree in the ground.

But roots do more than hold the tree in the ground. When rain falls and seeps down into the ground the water reaches the tips of the roots. On these root tips there are tiny roots that are as fine as hairs. They are called root hairs. Water from the ground gets into the tree through them. This water carries food material from the ground that the tree needs. Water goes from the root tips to the littlest roots, then to the bigger roots, then to the bigger roots, until it gets to the biggest. Then up, up it goes into the tree trunk.

Branches grow from the tree trunk. The branches get smaller and smaller until they are small, thin twigs. These twigs hold the leaves. When the water has climbed up the tree all the way from the root hairs to the leaves it has reached the end of its journey.

Veins carry water into the leaves

If you could see inside the roots and the trunk and the branches and the twigs you would see the small pipes that carry the water. If you look at the leaves of trees you will see the tiny veins that carry the water into the leaves. The needles on pine trees are its leaves. The veins are easy to see in large flat leaves. They are harder to see in pine leaves, but they are there just the same.

Roots get longer at their tips. So do twigs. Look at the ends of twigs in the spring and you will see the buds. Some of these buds are flower buds. When they open, the tree is full of flowers. Some are leaf buds. When they open, the tree is covered with leaves. If you watch leaf buds for a week or so you will see new leaves, and then you will see that the stem of the new twig is growing longer. The new part is fresh and green.

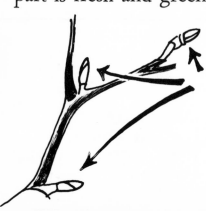

New twigs grow from here

last year's growth

new growth

←bud

If you look carefully at the end of the branches of your Christmas tree you will see which part is the newest. It's the freshest and the greenest.

A leaf is really a factory! It makes food for the tree. It makes food from the water that comes up from the ground and from a gas called carbon dioxide (KAR-bon di-OK-sid) that comes in from the air. Tiny holes in the leaves let in the carbon dioxide. The tree needs two other things or its factory will not make food. It needs a green material called chlorophyll (KLO-ro-fill). There is chlorophyll in the leaf. That is what makes the leaf green. The leaf also needs sunlight. The sun shines on the green leaf factory and the factory puts water and carbon dioxide together and makes food. This happens in flat leaves like oaks and maples, and it happens in the needle leaves of trees that make good Christmas trees.

Green leaves make food for trees out of carbon dioxide and water. They need sunshine and chlorophyll.

Oak leaves make food for oak trees. Pine needles make food for pine trees.

The tree uses this food to grow just as you use food to grow. The food helps the roots grow larger and longer. It helps the buds grow and make new twigs that make new leaves that make more food. The tree keeps making more food as long as the tree lives. That is what happens to make a tree grow large enough to be a Christmas tree.

Just under the bark of the tree is the place where the tree grows larger around. If you could see this place under the bark you would see that it is a fresh green layer. Every year the tree trunk adds another layer. When the tree is cut down you can see these layers. If you count them you can tell how old the tree is. There is one for every year that the tree grew.

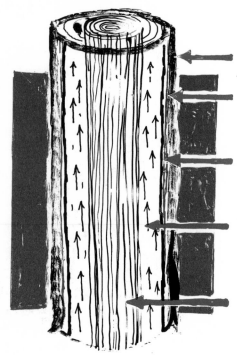

the outer bark protects the tree

the *cambium* is the growing layer of the tree

the inner bark carries food from the leaves back to the branches, trunk and roots

the sapwood carries sap from the roots to the leaves

the heartwood - which was sapwood once - gives strength to the tree

Which part of a tree is most important? Is it the roots, that hold the tree in the ground and take in the water and carry it to the trunk? Is it the trunk and branches, that carry up the water and hold the leaves in the air and sunshine? Is it the leaves, that make food from carbon dioxide and water? Is it the chlorophyll in the leaf? It takes all of these together as well as sunshine and rain to make a tree grow. They made your Christmas tree grow. They make all Christmas trees grow.

USING TREES FROM THE FOREST

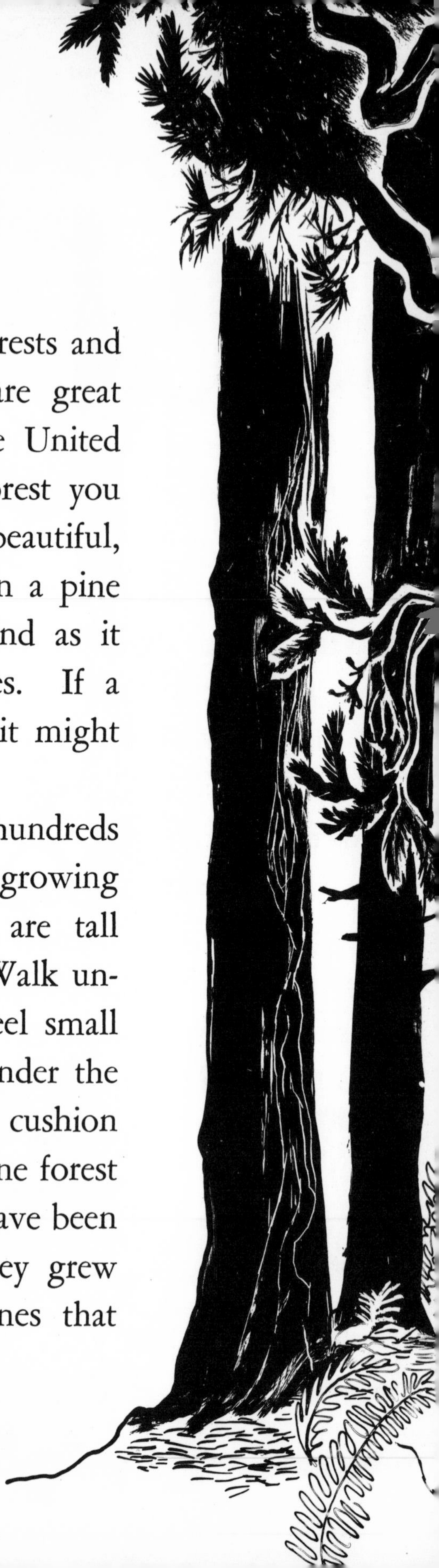

Christmas trees grow in forests and so do other trees. There are great forests in many parts of the United States. If you walk in a forest you will probably say, "This is a beautiful, quiet place." If you listen in a pine forest you may hear the wind as it hurries past the pine needles. If a forest could tell about itself it might say:

"I am a forest. I grow hundreds of trees. Some have been growing for years and years. They are tall and straight and beautiful. Walk under the trees and you will feel small for they are so tall. Walk under the trees and you will feel a soft cushion under your feet, for I am a pine forest and for years and years trees have been dropping their needles as they grew from small trees to large ones that point high to the sky.

"Look up and you can hardly see
the blue of the sky, because the tops
of the tall trees hide it. You will look
up and up and up before you see the
first branches of these old trees. Each
year the trees grow taller as they reach
for the sunshine. Each year they
grow larger around, too. Some trees
are so large no one's arms are long
enough to reach around them."

What happens to trees in a forest? If no one drops a match to start a fire they will keep on growing taller and bigger around. If people are careful to put out their campfires the forest will keep beautiful. If insects do not eat the tips of the branches where the trees grow longer the forest will stay beautiful and grow to be very useful. If there is plenty of sunshine and rain the trees will grow and grow.

Everybody uses the things that are made from the trees in a forest. Some trees are used to make paper—paper to write on—paper to make books— paper to make magazines and news- papers—paper to wrap things in like Christmas presents—and paper for dozens of other useful things. A sign on a forest might say:

Books and Magazines are growing here

and other things too

Some of the other trees from the forest are taken to a saw mill and made into flat boards and strong timbers that are used to build houses—houses to live in—floors to walk on—doors to open and close—roofs to keep out the rain. A sign on a forest might say:

Houses are growing here

and other things too

The tallest, straightest trees make fine poles—telephone poles to carry telephone messages—utility poles to carry electric wires—flagpoles to hold the flag high up in the breeze over schoolhouses and post offices and other places. A sign on a forest might say:

Poles are growing here

and other things too

A forest is a nice place even when it's raining. Under the trees the water drips softly to the earth. It runs down the branches to the trunk and seeps into the ground. In an open field rain splashes on the ground, hurries away, and often carries the land with it. It carries some of the food material that plants need away with it, too. Plants cannot grow in soil if the food material is carried away. But rain in the forest goes into the ground. The roots of the trees hold the water and the food materials. Forest soil is good soil. A good sign for a forest might be:

Here are water and soil savers

The woods where Fox Squirrel lives is a fine home for animals. Squirrels and other animals build houses high in the branches of the trees. Birds nest in the trees. They eat insects and they sing. Deer live among the trees. They can find food and they can raise their families in the thick woods and hide their young fawns there.

In winter when the wind blows hard and snow falls and it is so cold that water freezes to ice, birds find shelter in the thick branches of evergreen trees. Other animals live under the carpet of pine needles and in holes in the ground. Fox squirrels, and chipmunks and small mice find cones and other seeds to eat. A sign on a forest might say:

The sign on Mr. Ball's woods might say CHRISTMAS TREES ARE GROWING HERE, for in his woods there are cedar trees and fir trees and spruce trees that make good Christmas trees. They are called evergreen trees. There are many other kinds of evergreen trees. They do not drop all of their leaves in autumn as many other trees do.

An evergreen forest is green all winter. Evergreen trees drop a few needles at a time and keep on growing new ones. Maples and poplars and many other trees drop their leaves in autumn and then their branches are bare, but evergreen trees are always green.

In one year more than 25 million evergreen trees were cut for Christmas in our country. Most of these trees grew in forests. In many of these forests the trees grew close together. If these trees were all left to grow large there wouldn't be room for them. So when some of them are cut there is enough room for those that are left. They keep on growing and may be used for other things.

Some of our Christmas trees are grown on Christmas tree plantations. In these plantations the trees are planted and grown just to be cut for Christmas. When the trees are big enough and are cut for Christmas, new ones are planted. The Christmas tree farmer always keeps a new crop of Christmas trees growing. A sign on a Christmas tree plantation might say:

Christmas Trees are growing here. Merry Christmas!

longleaf pine is
generally used for
Christmas garlands

CHOOSING A CHRISTMAS TREE

Barbara and Billy had a hard time deciding what
kind of a tree they wanted, because there were many
kinds of evergreen trees in Mr. Ball's woods.

Many people like Douglas fir or balsam fir trees.
Some people like red cedar, some like black spruce
trees, and some like Scotch pine or white pine. Some
people don't know one evergreen tree from another.
Look at the pictures here and you will see what some
of the evergreen trees look like.

red
spruce

blue spruce

balsam fir

Scotch pine

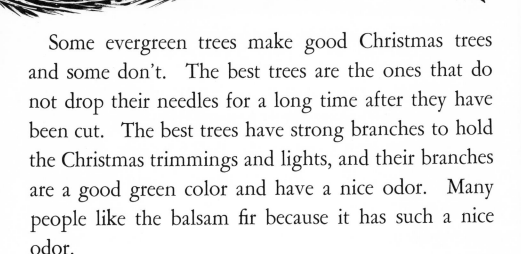

Some evergreen trees make good Christmas trees and some don't. The best trees are the ones that do not drop their needles for a long time after they have been cut. The best trees have strong branches to hold the Christmas trimmings and lights, and their branches are a good green color and have a nice odor. Many people like the balsam fir because it has such a nice odor.

You can make your Christmas tree last longer if you take good care of it. It will stay green longer and it will smell nice longer if you sprinkle it with water a few times before you bring it into the house. Cut a piece from the bottom of the trunk and then set the tree in water. This will make it last longer, because water will go into the trunk and up the branches to the needles. This will help to keep the tree green and fresh longer.

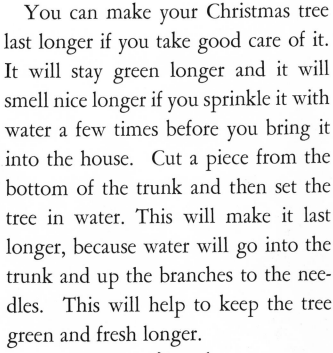

Red cedars are a kind of juniper. Their fruit looks more like berries than cones.

35

Look at the piece of wood that you cut from the end of the trunk of your Christmas tree. See the rings? Count them and you will know how old your tree is. There is one ring for each year the tree has been growing. Is your tree as old as you are?

Look at the ends of the branches of your Christmas tree. Can you tell which part of the tree is the newest part? Can you tell how much the tree grew last year?

Are there any cones on your Christmas tree? If there are cones, dry one of them and see if you can find the seeds. You might like to try planting them.

If you have a place to plant an evergreen tree you can have a living Christmas tree out-of-doors. Each year it will grow a little larger, just as you do. You can decorate it for Christmas, but it will be there all year. Many people have living Christmas trees. Some communities decorate a large growing evergreen tree and use it for a Christmas tree. Some schools plant evergreen trees in their schoolyards and use these living trees as Christmas trees.

MAKING A CHRISTMAS TREE FOR THE BIRDS

If you take good care of your Christmas tree it will still be fresh and green and beautiful after Christmas has passed. What can you do with such a beautiful, fresh green Christmas tree? You can make a Christmas tree for the birds that live near your house.

In winter, when it's cold and snow and ice cover the ground, birds have a hard time finding food. If you live where the winters are very cold and snow and ice cover the ground you can make your Christmas tree into a fine feeding place for birds. After Christmas is past, set the tree outdoors where you can watch it and put things on it that birds like to eat. Remember that some birds like seeds to eat and some birds like other things. If you want to make a tree for different kinds of birds you must put different kinds of food on it.

Get some suet from the meat market and fasten it to the tree branches. Nuthatches and woodpeckers like suet. So do some other birds.

Mix some peanut butter with some cornmeal so that it makes a paste. Put the paste into the holes between the scales of a large pine cone and hang it on the tree. Chickadees will enjoy this, and so will other birds. The cone makes a fine surprise Christmas package for birds.

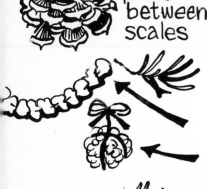

tie suet to branch

put peanut butter paste between scales

string popcorn or make popcorn balls

You will need something to hold seeds for the seed-eating birds. Here are pictures of some bird feeders that you can use. Fasten your bird feeder to the branches of the tree and you may see cardinals and bluejays and juncoes and other birds that like seeds.

a paper ice-cream cup makes a good feeder

so does a jar top

Pour a mixture of suet and wild-bird seed into an empty can, let it harden, then cut out the bottom so the birds can eat from both ends.

Some birds like raisins. Some like apples. Some like pieces of orange. Decorate the birds' Christmas tree with different kinds of things to eat if you want to see different kinds of birds.

You may need to wait a few days or even longer until birds find your tree. On snowy days they will certainly come, and you will say, "This is a good thing to do with a Christmas tree—especially after Christmas." And it is.

FINDING THE MOST BEAUTIFUL CHRISTMAS TREE

The National Community Christmas Tree in Washington, D.C., is a Christmas tree for Barbara and Billy and you and for all of the other people in the United States. You can see it at Christmas time near the White House. It is sometimes called the President's Christmas Tree.

Each year the great tree comes from a different state. Sometimes it is one kind of evergreen tree, sometimes it is another. One year it was a fir tree, from the state of Michigan. Another year a spruce tree was chosen, from South Dakota. Another year Minnesota sent the finest spruce tree it could find. Still another year Montana sent a beautiful spruce tree. And the states of Maine and Oregon have sent beautiful evergreen trees, too.

The tree that came from Montana grew by a mountain road near a rushing stream in the Rocky Mountains. For years people had seen the tree growing there and had often said, "This is a most beautiful evergreen tree. It has such a perfect shape."

Wild rose bushes and vines and other plants grew under the tree. Animals lived there. Birds made their nests in the great evergreen. In winter they rested in the thick branches to keep out of the wind and snow. Squirrels ran up and down its big trunk and gathered cones from its branches.

No one really knew how old the tree was. No one knew when the tiny seed that made it began to grow. But many people watched it get bigger year after year, and they loved the tree more and more. It grew to be nearly a hundred feet tall.

When the people began to look for a tree to send to Washington they thought of the wonderful spruce tree and said, "Of all the trees that are growing in our forest, this is the most beautiful. We will send it."

A woodcutter who lived nearby said, "I would like the honor of cutting the tree for the President of the United States. It is a fine thing for the state of Montana to send its most beautiful tree for so many people to enjoy."

On the day the tree was cut, a great snowstorm came to the mountain. It covered the branches of the tree and bent them to the ground. Snow covered the other forest trees and made deep drifts on the mountain. It was a very cold day.

A huge truck climbed slowly up the mountain road to the place where the tree grew. It carried a great derrick to lower the tree gently to the truck.

Many people watched as the woodcutter made a deep cut in one side of the tree. Then with a great saw he cut through the trunk. When the tree was cut the derrick slowly lowered it to the truck. As it began to fall, snow slid off the branches and flew in every direction.

"How old do you think the tree is?" people asked. They had tried to guess. "Now we will find out," the woodcutter said, and he counted the rings in the tree trunk. He counted fifty, and there were still more. He counted sixty. There were still more. He counted seventy and then nine more. "It took seventy-nine years for this beautiful tree to grow. And it took me only a few minutes to cut it down," the woodcutter said.

Men wrapped heavy cloth around the tree so that its beautiful branches would not get broken, and they fastened it to the truck. Then they started through the snow down the winding mountain road past the rushing stream to the railroad station. It took two huge railroad cars to carry the tree on its journey from Montana to Washington, D.C.

Finally the tree arrived in Washington. Trucks brought it from the railway station to the place near the White House where the National Community Christmas tree is placed. A derrick lifted it from the truck, and men fixed a platform to support it. When people saw the tree they said, "This is the most beautiful tree we have ever had. It looks like Christmas even without lights."

When the tree was ready, its green branches were hung with hundreds and hundreds of balls —red, blue, yellow, and silver. One gold star for every state in the nation hung on the tree. Bright colored lights were everywhere on the tree. There were seven thousand of them! At the very top there was a white star.

North, South, East and West,
people have many kinds of Christmas trees.

Every year, millions of
people enjoy the huge
Rockefeller Center tree
in New York City.

In the south, people often
decorate living palm trees,

and in the southwest
they sometimes decorate
Joshua trees.

In Seattle, Washington, a ship
carries a Christmas tree through
the waterways of the city.

In Hawaii, many people
decorate driftwood trees.
Cedar makes beautiful
driftwood.

45

Then, just before Christmas, the moment came to light the Christmas tree. Hundreds of people gathered around the huge evergreen tree in the nation's capital. Thousands of people from all over the United States turned on their television sets to watch the President of the United States light the tree. All at once the seven thousand lights came on. They shone on the red, blue, yellow and silver balls. The stars from the states lighted up. The white star at the top shone over the tree and over all the people. And the President and the people from far and near wished for Peace on Earth Good Will to Men. All through the Christmas Season people came to see the tree. Children sang and danced and were happy when they saw the tree.

When people looked at the tree they thought of many things. Some saw the lights and colored balls and thought, "This is indeed a beautiful sight." Some looked at the tall tree and the green branches and thought, "It is hard to believe that this great tall tree could grow from a seed smaller than a grain of rice." A forester looked at the tree and said to his friends, "You know, it's possible that a squirrel might have planted that tree." When Billy and Barbara saw the tree they said, "Even in our woods there is not a tree as beautiful as this."

Seventy-nine years of rain and sunshine had helped the tree grow to be nearly a hundred feet high. Each year the leaves made more food, the tips of the branches and the tips of the roots grew longer, and another ring was added to the growing trunk. This is the way of the Christmas tree. This is what happens before a tree grows large enough to be a Christmas tree. It happened to the tree that Barbara and Billy brought from the woods and it happened to yours.

CHRISTMAS
TREES
FOR SALE

Give me.
me.

VITAMIN A B1
Amoxylling
PARACENTAMOL
PAIN. RELIEF